ALLAH'S BEST FRIEND

Quran Stories for Little Heart

S A N I Y A S N A I N   K H A N

Designed and Illustrated by
Achla Anand & Achal K. Anand

Goodword
FOR KIDS

Goodword Books Pvt. Ltd.
1, Nizamuddin West Market
New Delhi 110 013
Tel. 435 6666 , 435 5454, 435 1128
Fax 9111-435 7333, 435 7980
e-mail: info@goodwordbooks.com
www.goodwordbooks.com

First published 2001
© Goodword Books 2001

D1247366

Long long ago, about 4000 years ago, in the faraway land of Iraq, a child whose name was Ibrahim عليه السلام (or Abraham) was born in the village of Ur.

He was so gracious, tender-hearted and pure in faith that Allah gave him wisdom when he was still a child.

Allah was so pleased with him that He made him His best friend.

6

Ibrahim's desire to find the truth grew. One night, while looking at the sky, Ibrahim علیه السلام noticed one very bright star. "This is my Lord," he said. But when it set, he said. "I do not love things which fade."

Then Ibrahim ﷺ noticed the moon shining brightly, as if it was made of pure silver. "This is my Lord," he said happily. But when it set, he said. "I do not love anything which sets."

After the same thing happened
with the sun, Ibrahim عَلَيْهِ السَّلَام
announced: "I will turn my face to
Him who has created the heavens
and the earth, and live a good life.
I am no idol-worshipper."

In the days of Ibrahim ﷺ, people used to worship stones and statues, but even as a child he wondered why.

Ibrahim's father, whose name was Azar, also believed in worshipping idols. When Ibrahim  asked his father why he worshipped objects that did not speak, Azar became angry.

One day, when Azar and the other townspeople were away, Ibrahim عليه السلام, took an axe and broke all the idols in the public temple except the biggest. When people discovered this, they asked Ibrahim عليه السلام, "Who has done this?" "Ask the biggest idol," replied Ibrahim عليه السلام calmly. "Why do you worship things that cannot even talk, move or understand?" Unable to understand the Prophet Ibrahim's message, they were left speechless. They became furious, and tried to kill him.

They suggested that since this boy had insulted their gods, they should burn him alive. A huge heap of firewood was piled up and set alight. The people shouted and chanted aloud: "Death to Ibrahim! Burn him!" They thought that the burning of Ibrahim  would cleanse their souls and protect them from harm.

As the bright red flames leaped up, Ibrahim  felt no fear, as his faith in Allah was very strong and he knew that the people were wrong. As soon as the fire reached its peak, they picked up the Prophet Ibrahim and threw him into the blazing fire. But Allah was with him. Allah commanded the fire, "O fire, be cool and peaceful for Ibrahim."

A miracle took place, and the fire, instead of burning Ibrahim ﷺ, became a cool, safe place for him. The onlookers could hardly believe their eyes! So awestruck were they that they could neither speak nor move!
The moral of the story is that faith in Allah is the only thing that can save a believer in this world and the world to come.

Find Out More
To know more about the message and meaning of Allah's words, look up the following parts of the Quran which tell the story of the Prophet Ibrahim ﷺ:
    Surah al-An'am 6:74-80
    Surah Maryam 19:41-50

ﷺ *Alayhis Salam* 'May peace be upon him.'
The customary blessings on the prophets.

24